# CELEBRATE U!!!

## THE PHENOMENALITY OF U

### BY

### DEBORAH R. HOUSTON

## A WOMEN'S DEVOTIONAL WORKBOOK

**This workbook is designed with U in mind ~**
**every girl, sister, girlfriend, home-girl, sorority sister, auntie,**
**grandmother, madea, and every female,**
**as we celebrate your extraordinary excellence in being the woman**
**that U are.**

**May it guide U to the**
**rediscovery of U.**

# CELEBRATE U!!!

# THE PHENOMENALITY OF U!!!

Everyday people find a reason to celebrate.
It's during these moments that we raise our glasses, kick up our heels,
clap our hands and lift our voices.
Our bodies respond with anticipation as we reach for our land-line or
cordless or cell phones, to make a quick call or to begin texting, not
while driving, or we feverishly click our fingers on computer keys to
spread our good news by way of the internet, making an
announcement to the world, in hopes that they, too, will join us in our
moment of celebration.

The reason or the event causing us to shout with glee or to even plan
and execute celebratory gatherings, for which we hope and expect
congratulations, range from the birth of a child, the passing of a class,
graduation, promotion, engagements, goals met, homes bought and
even the chartered course of new direction, yet, I believe that we
rarely take time to identify and celebrate what is most important, the
existence of ourselves  ~  the U, Me, Us, and We.

On this vast and enormous earth,  this globe,  this sphere,
there is no one quite like U.

U are unique.
U are one of a kind.
And guess what, there will never, ever be another U!!!

Why should there be?

No one can be and do U, better than U.

U are the original U.

No one should want to be U, nor should U seek to be another.


Everything that U need to be the best of your natural self,
was instilled upon your creation.
It's been with U since birth - deep down inside, waiting for the
moment, the clarity of mind and the acceptance
of yourself for yourself.

And once it's revealed, once you've decided to embrace the totality of
U, a fire is ignited, a reality of inner power is unleashed and a
completeness is achieved without the need of
additives or preservatives.

Without regret or remorse words are spoken to your soul, whispers of
words that cradle the very core of U and find it's resting place on your
heart, plucking it's strings that sends vibrations throughout every fiber
of your body and where there was once confusion, harmony of self now
reigns.  Whispers turn to words spoken as U converse with yourself,

giving way to a shout that has long been muffled.
A shout that has never been heard and gives birth to the voice that has
been waiting to make an announcement to the world that
U are worth celebrating.

That the occasion and the reason for celebration is simply spelled out
in one syllable ~ U!!!

And as we celebrate, who we are, we are given the ability to shift the
atmosphere, as we transcend from the average to the phenomenal ~
the wonderment, of U.
A woman, a being, and a creation that can never be fully explained,
harnessed or contained, but will forever be desired.

Today, and every day,
let us remember that there is a reason
to celebrate who we are, who we hope to be,
and who we will become.

Yet there's a bigger picture,
for the Celebration of U, filled with genuine love, joy and appreciation,
catapults U to the Celebration of others ,
not for the expectation of who U think they should be,
but for the totality of who they are.

Today, and the days to follow, I encourage U
to thank our God for His most phenomenal creation as we
Celebrate U!!!

Psalm 139:14
King James Version (KJV)

"I will praise thee;
for I am fearfully and wonderfully made:
marvellous are Thy works;
and that my soul knoweth right well."




Celebrate Your New Day




"The more you praise and celebrate your life,
the more there is in life to celebrate."

Oprah Winfrey

**Celebrate Your New Day**

Today is the beginning of your new day.

Your new life.

Your new direction.

Give thought to your experiences from yesterday and yesteryear, but do not set up house in them, rather, embrace the lessons of each, without regret, choosing to step into your today and anticipate the greatness of your tomorrow.

Speak life into your new day by reminding yourself that on this day and those to follow, U will not be tied to your yesterdays, your yesteryears or your past.

Today, U will learn from what has been and U will march forward to a destiny that has been prepared by God solely for U.

No longer will U linger in lackadaisicalness or muddle through the mistakes that have already been made.

What's done is done and it is what it is.

Today, U will stand as a woman full of the excitement of what this day holds  -   a new beginning, a fresh start and the first step into your tomorrows.

**Assignment:**

**Take the time to write down three valuable lessons that U learned about <u>life</u> from your yesterdays and yesteryears.**

_______________________________________________

_______________________________________________

_______________________________________________

_______________________________________________

_______________________________________________

_______________________________________________

_______________________________________________

_______________________________________________

_______________________________________________

_______________________________________________

_______________________________________________

_______________________________________________

**Write down three valuable lessons that you've learned about <u>yourself</u> as it relates to your yesterdays and yesteryears.**

_______________________________________________

_______________________________________________

_______________________________________________

_______________________________________________

_______________________________________________

_______________________________________________

Before we move forward, it's time for station identification...

Take an introspective look at the woman that U are.
We did not design our bodies, and there are only a few things that we can do to change how we look.

If U want to lose weight, do it!

If U want to change your style of dress, change it!

If U seek to cut your hair, cut it.

The outer woman is simply a reflection of what's going on inside of us.

In speaking to your inner woman, the real and natural U,
what would U change, if anything?

Is it a negative attitude, a nasty disposition, procrastination, struggling to finish what you've started, communicating skills, tired of being bullied, unable to forgive self, holding grudges, whatever the case, the power has been given to U to make the change to be better, to do better, to live better and to love better.


Given the list above and others that were not mentioned, what characteristics would U change about U?

_______________________________________________

_______________________________________________

_______________________________________________

_______________________________________________

_______________________________________________

_______________________________________________

_______________________________________________

_______________________________________________

**Now, that you're taking the first steps in shedding those things that have  been weighing U down, it's time to continue with the celebration of U!!!  For believe it or not, until U are able to acknowledge those things and make steps towards exterminating them from your life, U aren't truly able to embrace and celebrate who U are today for your tomorrows.**

Mark 11:25
King James Version (KJV)

"And whenever you stand praying,
if you have anything against anyone,
forgive him, that your Father in heaven may also forgive you
your trespasses:"




Celebrate Your Forgiveness




"The people who did you wrong or who didn't quite know how to show up,
you forgive them.
And forgiving them allows you to forgive yourself, too."

~Jane Fonda~

# CELEBRATE YOUR FORGIVENESS

There are two factors to forgiveness.

One, U have been forgiven.

Two, U hold the power to forgive.

The longer U choose to harbor feelings of discontent, the quicker your
spirit and soul are poisoned and so, today, this day,
U will make the wise decision to forgive.

Not only will U forgive the manner in which U feel U were wronged and
by whom, but it starts with U  -  your mistakes and your actions that
have hurt others and yourself.

U may not be able to forget; however, today, U refuse to make a point
to remember or to be bound by an unforgiving heart, for the refusal to
do so imprisons your spirit and handcuffs
the possibilities of your phenomenality.

He, she, and they don't have to say they're sorry, for hearing or not
hearing an apology from them doesn't dictate your ability to forgive.
Your action cannot be based on what they say or don't say.

U hold the power to forgive.

And today,
U will not allow someone else to take that from U.

**Assignment:**

**What are U holding against yourself?**
**What haven't U forgiven yourself for?**

________________________________________
________________________________________
________________________________________
________________________________________
________________________________________
________________________________________
________________________________________
________________________________________
________________________________________
________________________________________
________________________________________
________________________________________
________________________________________
________________________________________

**What grudge has weighed down your spirit like an anchor,**
**keeping U from moving forward?**

________________________________________
________________________________________
________________________________________
________________________________________
________________________________________

**From this day forward, make the conscious decision to exercise the**
**power to forgive; TODAY, not tomorrow.**

*Isaiah 40:31*
*King James Version (KJV)*

"But they that wait upon the LORD shall renew their strength;
they shall mount up with wings as eagles;
they shall run, and not be weary;
and they shall walk, and not faint."


Celebrate Your Strength


"A woman is like a tea bag —
you never know how strong she is until she gets in hot water."

~Eleanor Roosevelt~

# CELEBRATE YOUR STRENGTH

It's not necessary for U to flex your muscles or to strive to lift world record weight, for if truth be told, U have carried, shouldered, and had to bear more than anyone could ever imagine.

Your ability to do so has nothing to do with your size or outward appearance. It comes from your strength that abides within.

A strength that gives U the fortitude to stand when others would sit; to sit when others chose to stand; to speak when something needed to be said, and to even hold your tongue when necessary.

Believe it or not, U have more strength than U could ever admit. It's your strength that enables U to do what U do, and most importantly to be U, in all of your glory and phenomenality.
It takes more strength to be true and honest with yourself than to be a carbon copy of another, for the blueprint has already been laid.  Yet to have the audacity to be the authentic U, takes strength, for with each moment, U are learning and living.

Today, celebrate your strength  ~  instilled within, not only for yourself,  but also for those who are unable to find their own.

**Assignment:**

**Remember, we are marching towards the realization of our natural,
yet new born selves.
U are strong without measure, based on the power that lies within.**

**Realizing that U are destined to succeed in your life,
what  goals or dreams will require that U to tap within yourself in order
to exhibit strength?**

_______________________________________________________________

_______________________________________________________________

_______________________________________________________________

_______________________________________________________________

_______________________________________________________________

_______________________________________________________________

_______________________________________________________________

_______________________________________________________________

_______________________________________________________________

_______________________________________________________________

_______________________________________________________________

**U are your sister's keeper.  As we grow, change, learn, live and love, it
is important to share our life lessons with others, aiding them in the
realization of their power.  Write down the name of one woman that U
believe, at this time in her life, is unable to stand on her own and in
knowing this, U will make the choice and the decision to stand for and
with her, until she is able to stand on her own.**

_______________________________________________________________

*Proverbs 17:22*
*King James Version (KJV)*

*"A merry heart doeth good like a medicine:*
*but a broken spirit drieth the bones."*

## Celebrate Your Sense of Humor

*"Having a sense of humor has served me more than it has hurt me -*
*just in the sense that it has allowed me to keep my sanity."*

*~Dee Dee Myers~*

# CELEBRATE YOUR SENSE OF HUMOR

Your sixth sense.

Life, in itself, is serious.
Every day U are afforded opportunities that require U to be serious,
whether sitting in a corporate meeting or even various conversations.
However, every aspect of your life should not be so serious that U
refuse to find the humor in the funniest of things
that happen in your life.

Today, strive to possess the ability to be able to find humor in life and
even the ridiculousness of being your natural comedic self.

It is your ability to enjoy life as it is meant to be enjoyed.
Not through rose-colored glasses, but as it comes to U.

Humor keeps us healthy.

This doesn't speak of silliness or a moment of laughter at the expense
of another, for there's nothing funny about that.  Yet, if U take life as it
comes and find the humorous and even hilariousness of it, even days
that are overshadowed with gloom can be enjoyed.
And what at one time was considered a frustration can become a
head- shaking moment of laughter.

For example, I, like countless others, experienced a day when my to do list seemed unending and there didn't appear to be enough hours in the day.  Between meetings, I ran home to take care of more pressing business, before having to shortly leave.  I was ripping and running around the house, trying to be sure that everything was in place, when upon my trek to the door, I realized I didn't have my keys.  That meant I couldn't leave my home and I couldn't even start my car.  I spent the next hour searching high and low for my keys.  I tried to back track my steps, but there was nothing.  I was beyond frustrated.  Not only was I going to be late for my next appointment, but chances were that I might not make it at all.  I knew they were in our home, after all, I had just entered, but for the life of me, I couldn't remember where I had placed them.  I turned my purse upside down, spilling out the contents, but they weren't there.  I called my husband, knowing that he couldn't aid in telling me where they were, he wasn't even there, but I had to vent my frustration and he encouraged me to go back over my steps, which I did.

In doing so, I recalled placing my purse on the end table.  I retraced my steps to the kitchen and opened up the cabinets  -  nothing. I looked behind electronics  -  nothing, and even though I wasn't eating, I even checked the silverware drawers and still nothing.

In my frustration, I decided to get a drink.  I grabbed the glass and picked up the juice that was sitting on my kitchen counter, though I didn't remember putting them there.  When I decided to get some ice, to my amazement, there, in the freezer, were my keys!  I finally remembered wanting to grab something to drink upon entering my home and taking the necessary steps to do so.  During my search I was beyond frustrated, but at that moment, all that I could do was burst out into laughter at my comedic self.

**The next time your mind is weighed down with so many thoughts that U can't even think straight, make time to sit back for a moment and remember one of the most hilarious episodes in your life.  Write it down in as much detail as possible and enjoy the humor in it.**

John 8:32
King James Version (KJV)

"And ye shall know the truth,
and the truth shall make you free."

Celebrate Your Truth

"When we talk about putting ourselves first,
we are really talking about knowing our value.
You can't do that without understanding the truth
of who you are."

~Mikki Taylor~

# CELEBRATE YOUR TRUTH

One of the most difficult things for any individual is to be honest with
themselves  -  to see yourself for who U are
and to embrace what U see.

This can be extremely difficult if, during the course of your journey,
U have been surrounded by those who were either unable or unwilling
to supply U with the necessary tools to embrace the beauty of U and,
therefore, instilled within U feelings of inadequacy based on their own.

But today, the buck stops here!

No longer will U hide behind what someone else has conjured up in
their minds for U to be.

No longer will U tell yourself and agree with the untruths
about U.

No longer will U hide behind the facade of who U even  think U are.

Today U will embrace the truth of who U are,
in all of your phenomenality,
glory and splendor.

For the truth of the matter is, U are simply remarkable!

**Assignment:**

**Be honest with yourself.**
**What have U been telling yourself about yourself that denies U the ability to embrace who U really are?**

**This may not be easy to admit, but the sooner U are able to do this for yourself, the better U will be for yourself and for others.**

_______________________________________________

_______________________________________________

_______________________________________________

_______________________________________________

_______________________________________________

_______________________________________________

**Now, ask yourself, what was it about the untruth that caused U to accept it, rather than embrace the truth of U.**

_______________________________________________

_______________________________________________

_______________________________________________

**No matter how bad it may appear to be, it will never be as tragic as denying yourself of the truth of U.**

*Psalm 33:20*
*King James Version (KJV)*

*"Our soul waiteth for the LORD: He is our help and our shield."*

*Celebrate Your Patience*

*Patience is the ability to idle your motor*
*when you feel like stripping your gears.*

*~Barbara Johnson~*

# CELEBRATE YOUR PATIENCE

Yeah, U had to stand in line a little longer than U wanted; sure the traffic was moving at a snail's pace and of course, when U walked on to the elevator, all of the buttons were pushed, causing U to have to stop at every floor before reaching your destination, but what's the hurry?  You've learned to take life as it comes, planning, executing and rolling with the rushing, swelling tide or the gentle, slow and easy-like-Sunday-morning breeze.

Remember, patience is a virtue and one that doesn't happen overnight, but with each day, you're definitely getting there.

So, yeah, there's been a snag in your plans that have caused U to have to be patient.  If U can do something about it move things along, but if not, sit back and enjoy the ride.

If you're waiting for something, if it's truly worth it, U will savor it even moreso once it arrives.

If someone's waiting for your arrival, if they're aware of your phenomenality, then they'll realize that you're worth the wait.

**Assignment:**

**Did anything happen today that required your patience?**

**Ask yourself this...**

**If U found yourself waiting, was it worth the wait?**

**If not, don't allow yourself to be placed in that position again.**
**Patience is a virtue but time is also precious.**
**Also, be careful not to abuse the patience of others by placing them in**
**a position of having to constantly wait for U.**

**If U weren't pleased with the way U handled your patience today, what**
**would U have done differently?**

____________________________________________________

____________________________________________________

____________________________________________________

____________________________________________________

____________________________________________________

____________________________________________________

____________________________________________________

____________________________________________________

____________________________________________________

____________________________________________________

____________________________________________________

____________________________________________________

____________________________________________________

____________________________________________________

____________________________________________________

____________________________________________________

____________________________________________________

Psalm 139:7-10
King James Version (KJV)

"Whither shall I go from Thy spirit?
or whither shall I flee from Thy presence?

If I ascend up into heaven, Thou art there:
if I make my bed in hell, behold, Thou art there.

If I take the wings of the morning,
and dwell in the uttermost parts of the sea;

Even there shall Thy hand lead me,
and Thy right hand shall hold me."


## Celebrate Your Location


"If the sight of the blue skies fills you with joy,
if a blade of grass springing up in the fields
has power to move you,
if the simple things of nature have a message
that you understand,
rejoice, for your soul is alive."

~ Eleanora Duse~

# CELEBRATE YOUR LOCATION

From where you're standing, the view may not be pretty and then
again, the landscape may be perfectly manicured with the sunset
in the horizon.

Wherever U are right now, this is exactly where U were meant to be.
This is where U need to be.  For some reason, your location was
destined for U to learn something while here, so lean into the scenery
and learn to live in the moment.

That calls for U to be 'all in' wherever U are.
Not dreaming of the past or wishing for the future to the point where it
keeps U from being effective in the here and now.  If talking with a
friend, be there in the conversation, fully engaged; if working on a
project, devote yourself and time to doing just that, not allowing
yourself to be easily pulled away from the task at hand  -  embrace
where U are and savor the moment.  If you're not able to do that, then
move.  If U can't be fully engaged, admit it to yourself and others —
your time and their time is too precious to forfeit.

If U weren't meant to be where U are, simply stated, U wouldn't find
yourself at this place in your life.  No sense in complaining about it,
for your being here, may be about more than U.
U never know who U may encounter and the blessing that U can give
for having passed this way.

**Assignment:**

**Write down three things that U love about the scenery of where U are right now.  You'll be amazed at the beauty around U, once U actually take the time to look at it.**

**Embrace it for U may not pass this way again.**

**Number One:**

________________________________________________

________________________________________________

________________________________________________

________________________________________________

________________________________________________

________________________________________________

________________________________________________

________________________________________________

**Number Two:**

________________________________________________

________________________________________________

________________________________________________

________________________________________________

________________________________________________

________________________________________________

________________________________________________

________________________________________________

## Number Three:

___________________________

___________________________

___________________________

___________________________

___________________________

___________________________

___________________________

___________________________

___________________________

*Psalm 28:7*
*King James Version (KJV)*

*"The LORD is my strength and my shield;*
*my heart trusted in Him, and I am helped:*
*therefore my heart greatly rejoiceth;*
*and with my song will I praise Him."*

## Celebrate Your Song

*"If I love a song, I make it mine."*

*~Chaka Khan~*

# CELEBRATE YOUR SONG

Rhythm and blues, country, classical, gospel, rock and roll, rap, heavy metal or reggae!  Your toes tap, fingers snap, your head nods and your body dances, alone or with your partner ~  it's your song.

It's that song that when U hear it, your soul begins to smile and soar at the same time.  It's that song that takes your mind back to a specific place and time of your life when all was well and if not now, all will be well again.

Sometimes U sing along, allowing your voice to tackle notes and runs that the artist or instruments perfected.  Other times, U listen in silence allowing the notes to infiltrate your being as your heart beats in harmony and your body sways to the rhythm.  Regardless, it's your song, and  as it resonates with your soul U can feel it from the top of your head to the soles of your feet.  This song belongs to U and therefore, you've placed your stamp of approval and ownership on it.

Sure, others may claim it as their own as well, and U may willingly share it with them, but the experience that the song acknowledges belongs to U and U alone.

It is your song!!!

## Assignment:

Play your song.  Sing along to the top of your lungs or listen intently to every note.  Turn up the volume and celebrate your song.

Write down the titles of three songs that hold special meaning for U and why they hold a special meaning in your life.

**Song #1:**

_______________________________________________

**Reason:**

_______________________________________________

_______________________________________________


**Song #2:**

_______________________________________________

**Reason:**

_______________________________________________

_______________________________________________


**Song #3:** _____________________________________

**Reason:**

_______________________________________________

_______________________________________________

*Psalm 36:7*
*King James Version (KJV)*

*"How excellent is Thy lovingkindness, O God!*
*therefore the children of men*
*put their trust under the shadow of Thy wings."*

## Celebrate Your Shadow

*"To light a candle is to cast a shadow."*

*~Ursula K. Le Guin~*

# CELEBRATE YOUR SHADOW

No one else can claim your shadow.

It's attached to U.

Wherever U go, it longingly follows behind, quietly awaiting your lead
and supporting your path.

It is there, wherever U are, not to escape,
but rather to bring shade or relief to another.

Truth be told, U never pay much attention to your shadow.
As a matter of fact, your shadow never seeks your attention.
Your shadow doesn't holler, scream, jump or shout.
It never argues with U or seeks to be separated from U,
for it is a part of U and when others have walked away,
it remains, waiting for your next step, your next movement,
shuffle and even dance.

Today, celebrate and salute your shadow
and praise its' existence,
for to see your shadow means that U are standing in
and facing the sun.

**Assignment:**

**Your assignment is two-fold:**

**1)  Find some sunshine or a light source and
celebrate your shadow!!!
Go ahead, stand there, while the sun bathes U.
Now, look at your shadow.
Watch your shadow as it moves with U.
How about a round of applause.
U are applauding your shadow and your shadow is applauding U.**

**2)  Not everyone is able to appreciate their shadow.
Not everyone is ready to own the existence of their shadow and that it
simply comes from standing in the sun,
for they've been overcome by life's stuff, so much so, that they can't
appreciate the moment for what it is, an opportunity to simply be —
to exist.
Your shadow can serve as relief to another
who needs to be rejuvenated.
Today, be a shade of relief to someone who needs your help.**

*Joshua 24:15c*

*King James Version (KJV)*

*"…but as for me and my house, we will serve the LORD."*


**Celebrate Your Family**


*"Tennis is just a game, family is forever."*

*~Serena Williams~*

# CELEBRATE YOUR FAMILY

Mother, father, sister, brother, auntie, uncle, cousins, grandmothers, grandfathers or madeas, whether adopted or on loan, they were given to U to help to mold and shape your person.

It could be that those U hold dear and consider to be family, do not hold a DNA tie to that of your own, but family is much deeper than blood, for its common goal and focus is the best interest of U.

Maybe those who share your DNA weren't able to be there for U in the manner in which U would have liked for them to be, or as they should've been.  Even then, U are able to learn how not to be and what not to do in the forming, raising and dealings of your own family.

For those within your family circle, hear them, listen to them, glean from them, love them, appreciate them, learn from them, talk to them, share with them, help them, hold them and pray for them.

For when others may not give U the time of day, when you've left the nest and even branched out on your own, there is always a place to which U can return.  This place may not have an address or exist on a particular street, but it is the place where those who U consider to be your family dwell ~ a place called home.

**Assignment:**

**Select a family member that U haven't talked to in a long time and write down their name.**

_____________________________________________

**Call them just to let them know that
U were thinking of them.**

**You'll be surprised at the similarities that U share.**

**They'll be happy that U called and you'll feel better for doing so because just as U need to hear their voice, they are just as happy to hear your voice too.**

**Make a promise to keep in touch from this day forward.**

**They are your family...**

**Celebrate their triumphs,
cradle their cares
and commit to communicate.**

*Genesis 1:31*
*King James Version (KJV)*

*"And God saw every thing that He had made, and,*
*behold, it was very good."*

*(Yeah, that includes the chocolate which is made from the cacao tree!)*

Celebrate Chocolate

*"Sometimes a girl's gotta have some chocolate!"*

*~Carrie Underwood~*

## CELEBRATE CHOCOLATE

What woman doesn't love chocolate?

I'm sure there are a few, but, in this case, the majority rules.

Whether formed in the shape of a Hershey's kiss, filled with peanut butter or various shapes, sizes and neatly wrapped in a heart shaped box, it's the combination of the milk and the rich cocoa along with the occasion for its' consumption that warms U from within.

There's just something comforting about chocolate!!!
The flavorful ranges of deep-dark chocolate to milk chocolate or even white chocolate is nothing short of amazing.

The occasion could be a simple caffeine craving to a romantic gesture, but whatever the reason enjoy it by sipping, unwrapping or savoring it and salute your inner love for it.

**Assignment:**

**Girl, grab that hot chocolate, cocoa latte' or candy bar
and get busy.**

**U may even want to share it with someone special,
but don't let them have too much,
this is an about U moment  ~  U and your chocolate.**

*2 Corinthians 5:17*
*King James Version (KJV)*

*"Therefore if any man be in Christ, he is a new creature:*
*old things are passed away; behold, all things are become new."*

## Celebrate Your Starting Over

*"It's humbling to start fresh.*
*It takes a lot of courage.*
*But it can be reinvigorating.*
*You just have to put your ego on a shelf & tell it to be quiet."*
*~ Jennifer Ritchie Payette~*

# CELEBRATE YOUR STARTING OVER

Some may equate your reason for starting over due to the failure of something that you've tried, but that's not true.

How else were U to know that what U were attempting was not for U? It was your willingness to try, to make the effort and then to have enough sense to stop trying through your admittance that whatever it was and even whoever it was, was best left alone, in order for U to move on.

U haven't failed  -  and even if U feel as if U did, failure is never final, because what you've actually done is open the door to clarity leading U in a new direction.
Now, U can say that you've been there, you've done this, you've purchased and worn the T-shirt, but now your phenomenality has outgrown its' size and possibilities and U need not pass this way again.

Now you're ready to start anew, refreshed, and with a renewed spirit for the journey ahead.  You're not bitter, nor do you feel as if you've wasted your time.  This was a necessary and valuable experience which has afforded U the opportunity to weed out those things that will hinder U or waste your time in the long run.

And check it, your new start is going to take U over and beyond anything that U could've ever imagined.

Enjoy the journey, keep moving forward and higher.

**Assignment:**

**Identify one thing in your life that U continue to hold on to that's really keeping U from moving forward.**

**Ask yourself if it's worth holding on to and if not, put it down right now and ask for God's assistance in letting it go.**

**Your identification of this one thing will require that once U have decided to be done with it, U refuse to take it back.**

**U are purging it from your life.  It is of no value to U and it hinders U from the first step into your new direction.**

**Identification of the hindrance:**

_______________________________________________

_______________________________________________

**What caused U to hold on to it and what do U believe U were gaining by keeping it?**

_______________________________________________

_______________________________________________

_______________________________________________

**Are U going to throw it out or pass it on to another?  If you've been holding on to it, did it have value and if so, will it be valuable to another?**

_______________________________________________

*Proverbs 29:18*
*King James Version (KJV)*

*"Where there is no vision, the people perish:*
*but he that keepeth the law, happy is he."*

*Celebrate Your Passion*

*"Every great dream begins with a dreamer.*
*Always remember, you have within you the strength, the patience, and the*
*passion to reach for the stars to change the world."*

*~Harriet Tubman~*

# CELEBRATE YOUR PASSION


There's something that U love to do.

So much so that if it were up to U, you'd find a way to do it all of the time and wouldn't worry about payment.

U would dedicate every waking moment to it's success because it is such a part of U.

It burns within your soul, it keeps U up at night, it fuels your actions and U can't wait to bring your passion to the world.

U eat, breathe, sleep and taste the power of your passion.

U know that as soon as what lies within U is unleashed, the world will become a better place.  For U know that it will have a positive impact on those U encounter and those who are touched by your passion.

Don't allow the embers of desire concerning your passion to fizzle, fade, be shushed, silenced or blown out by another.

Let it burn, let it burn, let it burn.

Make a difference with your passion by using what lies within U for the betterment of another.

**Assignment:**

**What is your desire?**

_________________________________________________

_________________________________________________

_________________________________________________

_________________________________________________

_________________________________________________

**What is your dream?**

_________________________________________________

_________________________________________________

_________________________________________________

_________________________________________________

_________________________________________________

**How can U take your desire, your dream, which is your passion,
and change this world in a positive way?**

_________________________________________________

_________________________________________________

_________________________________________________

_________________________________________________

**The world has been waiting for U  ~  It's time to get busy!!!**

Job 14:14
King James Version (KJV)

"...all the days of my appointed time will I wait,
till my change come."


Celebrate Your Adaptability

"...We do not reject our traditions, but we are willing to adapt to changing
circumstances, when change we must.
We are willing to suffer the discomfort of change
in order to achieve a better future."

~Barbara Jordan~

# CELEBRATE YOUR ADAPTABILITY

As humans we are remarkable in so many ways.

One of these ways is our ability to adapt to our circumstances.

Think about it, there are stories of newborn infants who were discarded based on the shame of the immature mother who decided to leave them in horrendous conditions, yet that child survives; or the children who are raised in poverty and filth and rise above their surroundings; not to mention the adults who have been abused, yet are able to refuse to be defined by their pain and grow to do remarkable things.

No matter what has transpired in your life, no matter where U find yourself, whether U were able to land on your feet, or had to get back up and dust yourself off, U were able to adapt to your surroundings and U made the best of the situation.

Sure, it wasn't easy, no one said that it would be.
Yet here U are ~ still standing

If U were given lemons, U made lemonade.

If U found yourself in the heat of the kitchen, U found that U could stand it and U didn't run.  Instead U started cooking.

If the frigid winds started to blow, U bundled up, strapped on your galoshes and kept moving.

U didn't allow your surroundings to dictate your inability to succeed and just when others thought U couldn't handle it, U allowed your phenomenality to rise to the surface and U did it again  ~  adapted to the situation, made the necessary changes in order to survive and didn't give up.

**Assignment:**

**For some reason, there's something that you've been wanting to change about U.**

**It could be your hairstyle, your daily routine, U may even be thinking of changing careers...**

**Give it a try.**

**Wherever U land, you'll adapt and you'll succeed.**

**U are that phenomenal!!!**

**In what one area of life are U willing to take a chance on changing and therefore adapting?**

________________________________________

________________________________________

________________________________________

________________________________________

________________________________________

________________________________________

________________________________________

________________________________________

________________________________________

________________________________________

# Celebrate Your Haters

*Matthew 5:44*
*King James Version (KJV)*

*" But I say unto you, Love your enemies, bless them that curse you, do good to
them that hate you, and pray for them which despitefully use you,
and persecute you;"*

*"Be who you are and say what you feel
because those who matter don't mind
and those who mind don't matter."*

*~Dr. Seuss~*

*Romans 12:20*
*King James Version (KJV)*

*" Therefore if thine enemy hunger, feed him; if he thirst, give him drink:
for in so doing thou shalt heap coals of fire on his head."*

# CELEBRATE YOUR HATERS

**What?!?  Surely, you're kidding, right Debb?**

**Not at all.**
**Yeah, they bring hell to your door every chance that they get, and it would appear that they are on a mission to make your life miserable.**

**They set traps to ensure that U stumble, strive to sabotage your success, smile in your face while sneering inside and may even offer U an embrace hoping to get close enough to inflict pain with their instrument of harm .**
**Then if that's not enough they rejoice in your sorrow and take pride in being the culprit.**

**This individual does not have your best interest at heart.**

**But guess what, it's not even about them  ~  it's about U!!!**

**And their existence, their antics, their petty playing of elementary school mean girl games, simply shines the spotlight on U.**

**They are your advertisers and they don't even know it.**

**Haters motivate!**

**Haters see something in U that they wish they possessed and, based on the fact that U have what they want, their insecurities and immaturity causes them to look at U with disdain and campaign to get others to do the same.**

**Don't get caught up in their game.  As a matter of fact, pray  for them and thank them for the advertisement and the shout out!!!**

U don't hate them in return.  U actually feel sorry for them because they're unable to see the value that they can bring to life but they're too busy wasting time on watching your moves.

Today, choose to see them for who they are and what they do, take note and keep on stepping.

And based on who U are, you're able to greet them with a genuine smile for U are not defined by them.

Allow yourself to be fueled to elevation and motivation in order to reach your destination for God's glorification!!!

After all, if U weren't doing something right, the devils in hell wouldn't be trying to take U down!!!

**Assignment:**

**Knowing is half the battle.**

**1)  Identify your haters.**
**Now, don't get it twisted, don't place someone in this category**
**who doesn't belong.  If someone doesn't agree with U, has a**
**different perspective or isn't a friend, that does not mean that**
**they are a hater.**
**If you're honest with yourself, U know those who don't have your**
**best interest at heart and U may even know why.**
**Place their names on the blackboards of your mind.**
**However, be quick to take note and then erase it.**
**They need not take up more space in your brain**
**than they deserve.**
**2)   Always treat them with respect.**
**It always pays to be nice.**
**Don't allow their negativity to infect and then control your ability**
**to be your dazzling and phenomenal self.**
**3) Say a prayer.**
**Pray for them and make this a daily practice.**
**Your prayer should not be one of vengeance, but rather that they**
**will one day come to know and submit to the remarkability of**
**themselves, for in being the way that they are, though they may**
**never admit it, they are truly in a miserable state.**
**Then, say a prayer for yourself, as U deal with them in being your**
**best self and an example to them of phenomenality.**

Ecclesiastes 3:4
King James Version (KJV)

"…and a time to dance."


Celebrate Your Two-Step


"I hope you never lose your sense of wonder,
You get your fill to eat but always keep that hunger,
May you never take one single breath for granted,
GOD forbid love ever leave you empty handed,
I hope you still feel small when you stand beside the ocean,
Whenever one door closes I hope one more opens,
Promise me that you'll give faith a fighting chance,
And when you get the choice to sit it out or dance.

I hope you dance…I hope you dance…"

~Gladys Knight from Tyler Perry's The Family That Preys Together~

## CELEBRATE YOUR TWO STEP

Get up and shake your tail feather, girl!!!

It's your time to dance!!!

For too long, you've cared too much about what others would think
about U when their thoughts can't determine who U truly are.

This isn't about rhythm, it's not even about the song that's being
played, it's about U and your dance, your tango, twist, step, waltz,
jitterbug, bump, hustle and flow.

Get down with it, not because U want to but because U have to
for in doing so you're shaking off the funk
and whatever baggage U allowed to accumulate.

So, stop  being a wall flower, stop leaning against the wall and waiting
for someone to ask U to dance, and stop looking for a reason to dance.

If your dance is predicated upon the request of another or a reason
that may never come, U may be waiting a lifetime.

Get up, girl, DANCE!!!

Create your own soul train line and move!!!

If U need a reason, simply look in the mirror and celebrate
the woman that U are.

**Assignment:**

**Now ask yourself, when was the last time U danced?**

**Even if it was yesterday, get down with the get down.**

**If it's been a while, there's no time like today
to get your two-step moving.**

**Find your motivational song, crank it up and do your thang!**

**Whether in the kitchen, family room, or even doing a desk dance,
get down.**

**If you need a song to get U moving and your heart rate pumping,
try Tina Turner's, "Simply The Best",
Prince's, "Let's Go Crazy" or
Pharrell William's, "Happy".**

Jeremiah 29:11
King James Version (KJV)

"For I know the thoughts that I think toward you, saith the LORD,
thoughts of peace, and not of evil, to give you an expected end."

## Celebrate Your Purpose

"I truly believe that everything that we do and everyone that we meet is put in
our path for a purpose.
There are no accidents; we're all teachers - if we're willing to pay attention to
the lessons we learn, trust our positive instincts and not be afraid to take risks
or wait for some miracle to come knocking at our door.

~Marla Gibbs~

# CELEBRATE YOUR PURPOSE

**Don't get it twisted  ~  this is all about your purpose.  ~  not your passion, and there's a difference.**

**There are hundreds, if not thousands, of individuals who believe deep within their hearts that they are destined to be the world's next greatest singer, as they make their way to compete on a popular reality competition, such as   'American Idol'.**

**They have the passion, they sing with passion and it's that passion that drives and pushes them to compete, yet, when they open their mouths to sing and their notes snap, crackle and pop into the air, it's obvious that their passion does not coincide with their purpose.**

**U have a purpose.**

**There is a specific reason for which U were created.
It was given to U and instilled within U before U were born.**

**During your journey, your experiences in life are sent as a road map to your purpose.**

**The discovery of your purpose is found through persistent seeking and being in touch with who U are and not who others think U are or who they want U to be.**

**Know this...that when U walk within your purpose,
you're offering your service for the betterment of another.**

**Know this...that as U walk within your purpose,
U are secure in who U are.**

**Know this...that by living within your purpose,
U are confident in what was been placed within your care.**

**And it's that moment and that second, when what U <u>think</u> about your
purpose becomes what U truly <u>know</u>, that U are able to assist
another  in the discovery of her phenomenal purpose,
for U don't have to fear the loss nor the mistake of another trying to
take away what and who U are,
for it was given to U and U alone.**

**Assignment:**

**Do U know your purpose for being here?  If so, write it down.**

_______________________________________________

_______________________________________________

_______________________________________________

_______________________________________________

_______________________________________________

**How do U know ?**

_______________________________________________

_______________________________________________

_______________________________________________

_______________________________________________

**Are U living, walking, talking and breathing your purpose?**

**If so, U should also be helping another towards the rediscovery
of her purpose.**


**If not, what are U waiting for?**
**Don't allow what's been given to U go to waste  ~  get busy!!!**

*Proverbs 31:22*
*King James Version (KJV)*

*"She maketh herself coverings of tapestry;*
*her clothing is silk and purple."*

## Celebrate Your Style

*"I stay true to myself and my style,*
*and I am always pushing myself to be aware of that and be original."*

*~Aaliyah~*

# CELEBRATE YOUR STYLE

No matter what you're wearing, and despite the fact that the store
from which it was purchased had several others waiting to be snatched
up by other women in various sizes,  no one, and I mean no one,
can wear it like U.

No one can wrap that scarf , twist that hair, tie that bow, or even make
that jacket, skirt or suit swing the way that U do.

As a matter of fact, only U would think to put together the combination
of flair that boasts of your style.
Be it a hair clip, fingernail polish design or even the eyeglass frames
that adorn your face, it's U, all day, all the way.

It's your flair, the undeniable and unconscious original style that comes
forth in everything that U do, how U wear it, where U go and
when U work it.

Some may try to imitate it and duplicate it, but it was solely given to U
and so, try, though they may, they'll never possess your style,
for it is U and U are it.

Baby, flaunt your style; after all, U wear it well.

**Assignment:**

**Take a good look at U and admire your undeniable
and self-existing style.**

**Smile ~click~ and take a picture.**

**U are one of a kind.**

**Don't be afraid to try new things with your style; however, always
remember that your style speaks of U, and for U.
Therefore, your style should go with the flow of who U are.**

**Your style should always compliment the woman from within.**

Psalm 8:3-6
King James Version (KJV)

"When I consider Thy heavens, the work of Thy fingers,
the moon and the stars, which Thou hast ordained;

What is man, that Thou art mindful of him?
and the son of man, that Thou visitest him?

For Thou hast made him a little lower than the angels,
and hast crowned him with glory and honour.

Thou madest him to have dominion over the works of Thy hands;
Thou hast put all things under his feet:"


Celebrate Your Fingerprints


BILL CLINTON
OK?


"I want a fingerprint of my own and I want credibility, and that's all I
want.   I just want some substance to my existence."

~Lisa Marie Presley~

# CELEBRATE YOUR FINGERPRINTS

They were given to U as an identifier of your phenomenal self.

No one has your fingerprints, for they belong solely to U.

Whenever U touch someone, they receive access to what has been uniquely given to U by the Creator and is an identifier of U .

When U touch someone, they may not even realize it, but they've just received your branding and they will carry U with them as a reminder of your grace and inner beauty.

Your slightest touch leaves an undeniable signifier that U were there. It's a transfer of your energy and power and the release of your gift to have a positive impact and imprint on those U encounter.

Your fingerprints and your touch are so powerful that your presence remains even after U have departed.

**Assignment:**

**Have U ever really taken the time to look at your fingerprints ~
the miniscule grooves and the swirling design?**

**Each finger has its' own print and out of the millions, billions, and
trillions of people who have lived, are living and have yet to live,
none of them will have your fingerprints.**

**How amazing is that!?!**

**As U go throughout your day, be aware that your touch has power.**

**Your touch possesses the power to build up those in need and to tear
down the walls of denial for those who need to be reminded that their
unique design can make and have a positive difference in the lives
of all who we encounter.**

Jeremiah 17:14
King James Version (KJV)

"Heal me, O LORD,
and I shall be healed; save me, and I shall be saved:
for Thou art my praise."

Celebrate Your Scars

"I think scars are like battle wounds - beautiful, in a way.
They show what you've been through
and how strong you are for coming out of it."

~Demi Lovato~

# CELEBRATE YOUR SCARS

Everyone has at least one.

The scar may have been there for a while or U may have just received it, but to look at, to see it, takes U back to a painful moment. Because in order for U to have that scar means that U came in contact with and were close enough to something or someone that harmed U.

U were hurt.

The world may not even be able to see your scars but they are there, hidden from our view, but known to U.

Your scars may not be physical, but rather your spirit has been scarred and they have ruled your life, causing U to retreat within.

Regardless of their origin, to U they may seem hideous.
For U, they mar your beauty, inner or outer, and take away from what and who U are.

But, the fact that you have them speaks of your healing.
Despite the scars, whether external or internal, U still exist,
you're still here and U can still stand.

Today, refuse to be ashamed of them.
For too long you've allowed them to place a cloak over your phenomenal self.  Embrace them, accept them and even celebrate them for they are a part of U.  Don't allow them to speak on behalf of your abuse, anger or pain; rather, listen to their story of
strength, survival, and victory.

I have a particular scar that is associated with a painful memory.
I received it while running from something and in my haste, I clumsily connected with a window pane that shattered into a million pieces.  In my effort to get away, the pain that I should've felt from the cut didn't come until much later, after I had settled down.

At the time, the cut seemed so large and my body so small, but now my physical growth has caused the scar to appear very small,
yet it's still there.

And it's not going anywhere.

Yet, God has allowed me to outgrow what could've hindered me.
He has shown me that scars don't define me; they are simply a reminder of the ability to heal and to grow.

Now, if I look at it and I allow my mind to wander to the day of its' origination, I could become fearful and sad.
However, I choose to remember that just as that window pane has since been repaired, my pain has been healed and I'm still here!

**Assignment:**

**Look at your scars, inspect them if U must, but don't wallow in their origination for what happened yesterday was not sent to stifle U, but to strengthen U.**

**"Yesterday is in the tomb of time, tomorrow is in the womb of time, today is a gift, that's why we call it the present."**

**Celebrate your scars, for whatever caused them, though it could have destroyed U, U have been delivered.**

*Matthew 17:20*
*King James Version (KJV)*

*"…for verily I say unto you,*
*If ye have faith as a grain of mustard seed,*
*ye shall say unto this mountain, Remove hence to yonder place;*
*and it shall remove; and nothing shall be impossible unto you."*

*Celebrate Your Mountains*

*"You can't move mountains by whispering at them."*

*~Pink~*

# CELEBRATE YOUR MOUNTAINS

Your mountain appears larger than life itself.
It looms above U.
It stands in front of U,
daring U to make a move or to speak a word.
And it's not going anywhere until U make up in your mind and realize
that it does not define U.

It merely represents a challenge.
It's nothing more than an obstacle.
Perhaps larger than others, but its' size can't begin to equal the
phenomenal power that lies within U.

U possess the power to decide when to climb this mountain and when
to simply speak to it and watch it move
out of your way.

Should U choose to climb, know that each step and every strategic
placement of the grasp of your hand takes U higher, pushes U forward
and catapults U to an elevation of survival and before U know it, you'll
find yourself basking in the glory of the sun and clouds.

Perhaps this mountain isn't worth your climb, but simply requires the
power of your faith and your words.
The result is the same, for U will have conquered it by moving towards
your goal and destination
of being a better U.

Either way, whether U climb or speak, U will overcome!

**Assignment:**

**What is standing in your way?**
**Who is standing in your way?**
**Is it U?**

______________________________________________

______________________________________________

______________________________________________

**Whatever or whoever, first, have a conversation with yourself in order for U to be reminded of the power that lies within U.**

**Now, decide whether your power needs to be exhibited through your words, your actions or both.**
**One will take more time than the other, so choose wisely.**
**Whatever U decide, it will be for your betterment.**

**This is your mountain.**

**This is your power.**

**This is your moment to be a mountain-mover!!!**

*Proverbs 17:17*
*King James Version (KJV)*

*"A friend loveth at all times…"*

**Celebrate Your Sisterhood**

*"Lots of people want to ride with you in the limo,*
*but what you want is someone who will take the bus with you*
*when the limo breaks down."*

*~Oprah Winfrey~*

# CELEBRATE YOUR SISTERHOOD

They are your girls, your homies, buddies, bff's (best friends forever), sister girls, besties, confidants, trusted allies, girls-night-outers, prayer partners, breakfast, lunch or dinner meeters, shopping spree greeters, cry-together-Kleenex-eye-wipers, side-splitting-laughter-jokers, and talk on the phone friends.

When all else fails, U know that U can count on them. They're always ready to dispense advice, opinion and guidance based on what U need to hear, not necessarily what U want to hear. U may not agree with the advice given. U may even have a difficult time hearing their opinion, but U accept it for U know that they have your very best interest at heart.

This sisterhood consists of the friends that can finish your sentences, read your thoughts and see your expressions through the phone, and understands those times when words aren't necessary, but they will, instead, hold your hand in their heart because they understand the true meaning of friendship.

They know your secrets, accept U for who U are and love U even more.

They are your forever cheerleaders.

U know them, not the pretenders, the real deal friends.

Truth be told, U don't have many of them, but U know who they are and no matter where they are, near or far, each is held in the heart of the other.

**Assignment:**

**Write down the names of your three closest friends and why they are your closest friends.**

**This may take U back down memory lane, and in doing so, will cause U to cherish them even more than before.**

**Grab the tissues as U reminisce...good friends are the rare and valuable jewels of a lifetime.**

**Name:**_______________________________________________

**Reason:**______________________________________________

_______________________________________________________

_______________________________________________________


**Name:**_______________________________________________

**Reason:**______________________________________________

_______________________________________________________

_______________________________________________________


**Name:**_______________________________________________

**Reason:**______________________________________________

_______________________________________________________

_______________________________________________________

**Part II:**

Today, call them, tweet, Facebook, email or text them and let them
know how much U appreciate them, for they were given to U by God.

They are a blessing and a treasure that U should never,
ever take for granted.

Make plans to meet and get away.

Do more than make plans, do it.

And when U hook up for your girls get away, embrace one another with
genuine love for who U are to one another; spend the night talking of
your yesteryears; your plans, hopes and dreams for tomorrow  and
enjoy the time to laugh and be in the presence of one another.

Here's to the sistahs!!!

*1 Thessalonians 5:5*
*King James Version (KJV)*

*"Ye are all the children of light, and the children of the day:*
*we are not of the night, nor of darkness."*

## Celebrate Your Soul Glow

*"People are like stained-glass windows.*
*They sparkle and shine when the sun is out,*
*but when the darkness sets in,*
*their true beauty is revealed only if there is a light from within."*
*~Elizabeth Kübler-Ross~*

# CELEBRATE YOUR SOUL GLOW


There's an inner glow inside of U  ~  It speaks of your light.
It's a light that can only be dimmed by U.

When used properly, your light won't outshine another,
but it will ignite a spark within someone else.
Your acceptance of your soul glow will only enable your light
to shine brighter.

It's not about some school girl competition
or seeing who can cross the finish line first,
it's about helping one another to endure until the end.

However, let it be known that not everyone will be able
to handle your soul glow.
Some may even want to snuff it out,  encourage U to 'hide it under a
bushel' or deal with U based on their insecurities which causes them to
refuse to look within, offering U a questioning look of, 'who do you
think U are', but pay them no mind.

So, my dear phenomenal sister,
the choice for U to be the light that U can be for others to follow,
the choice for your soul to be warmed by it and to reach your full
potential in the wake of its' light is up to U.

Instead of co-signing the destructive behavior of others,
celebrate your inner glow.

Your soul must glow, it must shine,
it has to give light,
not as a spotlight to bring attention to yourself,
but rather as a lighthouse to inform others of their ability
to do the same.

**Assignment:**

**While U walk, when U talk and when U do what U do, remember who U are and that your light shines bright and lights the way for others to follow.**

**To what community cause can U  lend your assistance that will warm the inner glow of your soul and serve as an example for others to do the same?**
**Contact that community establishment today,**
**introduce yourself and see how your inner glow can spark a change in your community, city, state, nation and world.**

_______________________________________________

_______________________________________________

_______________________________________________

_______________________________________________

_______________________________________________

_______________________________________________

_______________________________________________

_______________________________________________

_______________________________________________

_______________________________________________

_______________________________________________

_______________________________________________

_______________________________________________

_______________________________________________

_______________________________________________

## Celebrate Your Smile

"I smile,
even though I hurt see I smile,
I know God is working so I smile,
Even though I've been here for a while I smile.
Smile, it's so hard to look up when you've been down,
Sure would hate to see you give up now
You look so much better when you smile, so smile."
~Kirk Franklin~

**CELEBRATE YOUR SMILE**


**U have been given a very unique and one-of-a-kind gesture
in which to greet the world.**

**Your smile!!!**

**When U smile, without greetings being exchanged or words being
spoken, your smile says volumes.**

**Your smile informs others that despite what's going on outside of U,
that all is well with your soul.**

**Even when U find yourself in the most awkward of situations or when
confronted by someone who insists on prying into your affairs with
uncomfortable questions, there is never a need to lose your kool,
raise your voice or even break a sweat, just smile.**

**Take a moment to gather your thoughts, clear your brain
and pull it altogether with an easy smile.**

**No need to cheese or grin, where every tooth you've been given is
noticeable ~ simply smile.**

**The world is waiting to see U smile.**

**The world needs to see U smile.**

**In doing so,
your smile will brighten the gloomiest of days for the brightness of
your inner glow shines forth in your smile.**

**Smile  ~  and watch the clouds dissipate.**

**Assignment:**

**Look in the mirror.**

**At first, don't smile.**

**Now, allow the corners of your mouth to gently lift.**

**It doesn't take much effort.**

**As a matter of fact,**
**U use more muscles in your face when U frown**
**than when U smile.**

**Show the world your beautiful, one-of-a-kind SMILE!!!**

**In doing so, you'll make someone's day as well as your own.**

Genesis 2:7
King James Version (KJV)

"And the LORD God formed man of the dust of the ground,
and breathed into his nostrils the breath of life;
and man became a living soul."

Celebrate Your Inhale & Exhale

"I wake up every day and I think,
'I'm breathing! It's a good day.'"

~Eve Ensler~

# CELEBRATE YOUR INHALE & EXHALE

The average individual takes approximately 17 million breaths per day.
Yet, as we go about our comings and goings and handle our business,
very seldom do we give thought to our breathing.

We don't spend our time counting them or keeping track of them,
we simply inhale and exhale.

Every breath that U take, in and out, should be celebrated.

One, it lets U know that U are alive, but each inhale and exhale
possesses a celebratory reason of its' own
because of what it stands for...

The inhale, to take something in, expands the lungs.
U are taking something in that gives U life and sustenance.
U are opening your heart for life to be enjoyed.

To exhale, is to rid your body of carbon dioxide.
U are removing what can and could be detrimental.
U know that U don't need it  ~ to hold it is of no benefit to U,
and so U expel that which can bring harm.

**Assignment:**

**Take a deep breath to cleanse your mind.**

**Slowly exhale in order to cleanse your body.**

**Inhale:**

**Give thought to one thing that needs to be cherished and embrace it.**

_______________________________________________

_______________________________________________

**Exhale:**

**Recognize one thing that needs to be expelled from your life.**
**There may be more than one thing but identify one thing that U are
ready to be rid of  today ~ right now.**
**If you're not ready to be free of it, then don't write it down.**

**Once you've identified one thing, wish it well, and exhale, thus setting
it free.**

_______________________________________________

_______________________________________________

*Matthew 14:23*
*King James Version (KJV)*

*"And when He had sent the multitudes away,*
*He went up into a mountain apart to pray:*
*and when the evening was come, He was there alone."*


## Celebrate Your Solitude


*"I had to learn - since I'm divorced now and everyone is like,*
*'Oh my God, you're single, what's going on?' -*
*that if I don't like to spend time with myself,*
*how can I ask someone else to enjoy spending time with me?*
*I'm getting to learn how to enjoy my solitude and have a good time."*

*~Gabrielle Union~*

# CELEBRATE YOUR SOLITUDE

When all is quiet and still  -  these are the times
for which your soul longs.

With the hustle and bustle, the push and pull and the
heave and ho of life,
U may not get the opportunity to be alone often.

As women, we are pulled in so many different directions that to find
time alone is rare.  There are always times when a phone call needs to
be answered or returned, breakfast fixed, lunches made or dinner
cooked, deadlines to meet or meetings to be scheduled.

Whether U are a domestic engineer, teacher, accountant, secretary,
banker, doctor, CEO, prosecuting attorney, judge or serving jury on
duty, whatever the career  or the usual tick tock of your everyday
clock, time to be alone can be few and far between.

Every now and then,
U may crave these quiet moments when it's just U,
all by yourself.
These are the rare moments when U can cuddle up
with a warm blanket,
a hot cup of tea and a good book that's been collecting dust while it's
been waiting to be read, or it could be that long relaxing bubble bath
with lights out, candles lit and no one else but U.

These moments are few and far between and may only last for five
minutes, so steal away and take advantage of it.
These times don't come by very often.

**Assignment:**

**When was the last time U were able to be alone, uninterrupted?
Has it been that long!?!**

**Write down the name of a book that you've had every intention of
reading but you've been too busy to do so.**

**If I may suggest a great read, "Father Knows Best"
by yours truly will inspire U!!!**

---

**Today, even if it's only for five minutes, take your time,
make some time and relax.
Shut down the cell, power down the computer or laptop,
turn off that television, or radio, and enjoy the silence of being in the
company of U.**

**Enjoy your moment of solitude for as long as possible.**

**Now, make time to do this more often.**

*Psalm 30:5c*
*King James Version (KJV)*

*"...weeping may endure for a night,*
*but joy cometh in the morning."*

*Celebrate Your Tears*

*"Tears are God's way of cleansing the heart."*

*~Rebecca Barlow Jordan~*

# CELEBRATE YOUR TEARS

Tears are shed for various reasons and therefore the evidence of them can mean different things  -  the birth of a child, witnessing wedding vows, grief as the result of loss, hurt feelings, overwhelming pain, the bearing of another's burdens, a touching moment that U witness while watching a movie, even the result of side-splitting laughter.

Your tears were given to U by God and for that reason,
they are worth celebrating.

To hold them at bay and to lock them within your soul is to deny yourself the opportunity of an inner exfoliation.
For after their release, U are cleansed and U are released from the pressure that has built up by allowing them to remain.

Despite what U may have been told before,
to release your tears is to exhibit strength that you've always had,
perhaps without your even knowing it.

U may have also heard that there's nothing like a good cry.
When one has been holding on and holding out, to allow the tear to be free cleans the soul, clears the vision and authorizes your claim to heal.

**Assignment:**

**Ok, so when was the last time U had a good cry, for whatever reason?**

**Remember, it's more about the release of the emotions than the reason for them, that allows your soul to soar for it has been set free from the pressure of holding on to the tears.**

**When was your last cry?**

_______________________________________________

_______________________________________________

**How did U feel afterwards?**

_______________________________________________

_______________________________________________

**How did others respond to your release of tears,
if they witnessed them?**

_______________________________________________

_______________________________________________

**How do U respond to others at the release of their tears?**

_______________________________________________

_______________________________________________

*Genesis 1:27*
*King James Version (KJV)*

*"So God created man in His own image,*
*in the image of God created he him;*
*male and female created He them."*


## Celebrate Your Reflection


*"If we want our daughters to honor their bodies,*
*they need to hear us honor ours,*
*no matter what size or shape we are,*
*no matter what scars or sags we see in that mirror."*

*~Regina Brett~*

# CELEBRATE YOUR REFLECTION

Your reflection is an undeniable and unenhanced look at U.

The mirror will never spare your feelings by presenting what's not there.

Again, it simply is what it is and it will be what it will be, unless U change it.

Whatever changes are made by U will be reflected in that mirror.

What U see is the beauty of your natural self.

Your reflection doesn't seek to make adjustments for U.

It leaves that up to U.

Your reflection doesn't seek to give U the view of someone else, for it is content in being U.

It won't run away from showing U who U are, but rather, your reflection gives U the uncut, unedited version of U.

And, my dear, U are beautiful.

**Assignment:**

**Stand in front of your mirror, covered or uncovered, the choice is yours.**

**Admire U for the woman that U are.**

**Remember, there will never, ever be another U.**

**Love U.**

**Embrace U.**

**Be U.**

Joshua 1:9
King James Version (KJV)

"Have not I commanded thee?
Be strong and of a good courage;
be not afraid, neither be thou dismayed:
for the LORD thy God is with thee whithersoever thou goest."


Celebrate Your Courage


"Courage doesn't always roar.
Sometimes courage is the little voice at the end of the day that says
I'll try again tomorrow."
~Mary Anne Radmacher~

# CELEBRATE YOUR COURAGE


It has taken a lot for U to be who U are, to do what U do and to be where U are  ~  to be comfortable in your own skin.

Some said you'd never make it, others may have said it was a waste of time and a waste of trying, and then there were those who discounted your ability and your reasoning.

But U never gave up on U.
Even if it took every ounce of courage, U did it.
When others decided to sit, U stood.
When others were too weak, U found the courage
to exhibit your strength.
When others muffled and stifled their own voices,
U spoke, cheered, yelled or screamed.
Even when they watched as silent partakers on the sidelines, perhaps
in the wrong doing of another, your conviction
teamed up with your courage
and U refused to be a cosigner of injustice.

No, it wasn't easy.
There may have been days when U may have found yourself by
yourself, but U remained steadfast in your courage.
Your courage burst forth as a rushing tide causing U to sit when
necessary, stand when prompted, speak if needed and to simply do the
right thing at all times.

**Assignment:**

**Write down an instance when U had to be courageous.
Write down your feelings during your courageous act.**

**Were U afraid to be courageous at that time?**

**How did U feel afterwards?**

John 8:36
King James Version (KJV)

"If the Son therefore shall make you free,
ye shall be free indeed."




Celebrate Your Freedom




"I like to be a free spirit.
Some don't like that, but that's the way I am."

~Princess Diana~

# CELEBRATE YOUR FREEDOM

U have been on lock down long enough.

U allowed yourself to be handcuffed to your past.

U allowed the simple-minded to incarcerate U
based on their insecurities.

U have been enslaved to deny yourself of who U are.

Enough is enough!!!

Today, U realize that U are free.

U are free
to decide,
to choose,
to progress,
and to live.

This is your emancipation moment
and U will never be harnessed again.

However, your freedom, as with all powerful things,
comes with a price.

The price of your freedom is your commitment and dedication to free
another, so that they can soar into the freedom that awaits them.

**Assignment:**

**What does freedom mean to U?**

_______________________________________________

_______________________________________________

_______________________________________________

_______________________________________________

_______________________________________________

_______________________________________________

_______________________________________________

_______________________________________________

**What or who has held U in a holding pattern,
keeping U from obtaining and embracing the freedom of who U are?**

_______________________________________________

_______________________________________________

_______________________________________________

**U were created to be free, to never be enslaved to anyone or anything,
not even to your own fears.
It's time to spread your wings and fly!!!**

Genesis 2:22
King James Version (KJV)


"And the rib, which the LORD God had taken from man,
made He a woman,"




Celebrate Your Curves




"I just had to grow to love my body,
I'm either going to love me or hate me.
And I chose to love myself."

~Queen Latifah~

# CELEBRATE YOUR CURVES

U are a woman.

A vivacious and curvaceous woman.

Each curve is a path that leads to who U are.

There's no need in trying to hide your curves.

It doesn't make sense for U to hate your hips,
belittle the bodaciousness of your bosoms
or shy away from your shape  -  it's U,
in all of your glory and splendor.

U were made to have curves and each one tells a story of the woman
that U are.

In essence,
your creation speaks of your curves.

They were given to U to enhance your beauty.

Be proud, be bold, be U!!!

**Assignment:**

The next time U jump out of the shower or the bathtub,
and after you've dried yourself off,
make your way to the mirror,
unclothed, unharnessed and uncovered
and take a good look at U.

Every curve...
the fullness of your cheeks...
slant of your eyes...
slope of your neck...
smoothness of your shoulder...
length of your arms...
tenderness of your tummy...
roundness of your rump-shaker...
power of your thighs...
delicate design of your calf...
angle of your ankle...
arch of your back...
and security of your secret garden...
every part of your body from head to toe
is a curve that leads from one to the other,
that equals the phenomenality of U.

*Ecclesiastes 3:4b*
*King James Version (KJV)*

*"...a time to laugh;"*

*Celebrate Your Laughter*

*"If you're serious,*
*you really understand that it's important that you laugh*
*as much as possible and admit that*
*you're the funniest person you ever met.*
*You have to laugh.*
*Admit that you're funny.*
*Otherwise, you die in solemnity."*

*~Maya Angelou~*

# CELEBRATE YOUR LAUGHTER

There's not another human being that possesses the sound
of your laughter.
The timbre in your laughter was created just for U and it can never be
duplicated by another, for U are its' owner.
It's release and sound is the result of the joy that bubbles and
overflows from the reservoir of your soul that can go from an infectious
giggle or guffaw to a whoop and even a holler.

The sound of your laughter is the result of a joke shared, a hilarious
moment or even the joy of your being U, for the side-splitting moments
of laughter are often a result of your comical self.

It's the sound of your smile in animation that, when heard, causes
others to wonder of its source and be reminded that wherever U are,
life can and is being enjoyed, just as it was meant to be.


My mentor and friend is the sole owner of the heartiest laugh
I've ever heard.

It's more than a chuckle or a giggle, it's a full-fledged, hearty,
from-the-gut, soul-sounding laugh that, when heard, has a language
all its' own that informs the hearer that she's enjoying her life.

To hear her laughter, actually brings a smile to my face
and even causes me to chuckle.

It's this laughter, the sound of it, that reminds me that life was meant
to be enjoyed as much as possible.

Laughter is good for the soul and the best medicine for a heart that
may be breaking or a pain that needs to be healed.

**Assignment:**

**Write down one of the funniest moments that you've ever shared in your life.**

**What happened?  Where were U?  Who were U with?**

**Never forget this moment and allow it to bring cheer to your heart and soul, should U ever need to be reminded.**

_______________________________________________

_______________________________________________

_______________________________________________

_______________________________________________

_______________________________________________

_______________________________________________

_______________________________________________

_______________________________________________

_______________________________________________

_______________________________________________

_______________________________________________

_______________________________________________

_______________________________________________

_______________________________________________

_______________________________________________

_______________________________________________

_______________________________________________

_______________________________________________

_______________________________________________

_______________________________________________

# Celebrate Your Accountability

Jeremiah 17:10
King James Version (KJV)

"I the LORD search the heart,
I try the reins, even to give every man according to his ways,
and according to the fruit of his doings."

"I see more people taking on the cloak of accountability,
more people tiring of the blame game..."
~Jane Sidberry~

Romans 14:12
King James Version (KJV)

"So then every one of us shall give account of himself to God."

# CELEBRATE YOUR ACCOUNTABILITY

It's always easy to take credit for the actions of which others approve, for in doing so, we receive a pat on the back, public adoration, and perhaps gazes of admiration.  Yet, to own oneself, to be accountable for who U are and what U have done requires the acceptance of not only the good, but also the bad and even the ugly.

Perhaps U made a mistake.
Maybe U said the wrong thing at the wrong time.
Then again, maybe U said the right thing in the wrong way.
It could be that your assessment, your judgment call or your perception was way off.  However, in thinking it was right,
U acted upon it and the result was hurt feelings, daggers being thrown and hearts being broken.  At least you're to the point where you're no longer playing the blame game, but today you're owning your mistake and you're on the way to making amends.

Whatever the circumstances, good, bad, ugly or indifferent, call this for what it is and own who U are and your part in whatever has transpired.

If U can change the situation for the better, then do so.

However, be true and honest with U, for U and for others.

Be accountable for who U are, what you've done
and always strive to be better.

**Assignment:**

**Write down an action for which U refuse to take accountability.**

_________________________________________________

_________________________________________________

_________________________________________________

_________________________________________________

_________________________________________________

_________________________________________________

_________________________________________________

_________________________________________________

_________________________________________________

_________________________________________________

_________________________________________________

_________________________________________________

_________________________________________________

_________________________________________________

_________________________________________________

**Why are U continuing to pass the blame on to another?**

**Own your part, your role, your decision, the words that came from your mouth or the actions that u decided to take.**

**Genuinely apologize, for even though U can't take it back,
U can be better  -  today.**

Romans 3:23
King James Version (KJV)

"For all have sinned, and come short of the glory of God;"




Celebrate Your Areas of Improvement




"Imperfections make you more beautiful"

~Beyonce~

# CELEBRATE YOUR AREAS OF IMPROVEMENT

All of us have those areas in our lives where we feel as if we could
and should be doing better,
whether pointed out by others or made aware by our own confession.

Procrastination, negativity, tardiness, overeating, exercising more,
finishing what U start, breaking promises, wasting time, listening
more, talking less...the list goes on and on.

It's these areas that speak of your humanity and confirm your
willingness to be catapulted to a higher, newer and better level of
yourself, for yourself and others.

In choosing to remain where U are,
U deny yourself the opportunity to grow, to learn, to be challenged and
to even conquer, for it's under the guidance of His hand,
that phenomenality awaits.

And it's not easy,
for to look at U and to see that there are areas in your life that need to
be made better, calls for a deep introspective look at who U are, where
U are and where U want to be.

It's shedding the veil that covers, hides and tucks things in.
The unveiling of these things leads to the revelation of them being
discarded or reconstructed.

Today, U will see yourself for who U are, and accept the challenge to be
better and to do better, knowing this is the path that leads to the
discovery of your phenomenality.

**Assignment:**

**U know what needs to be done.**

**U know what areas of your life need to be changed and U know why,
for to deny the improvement handcuffs U to a holding pattern.**

**What are these areas?**

---
---
---
---
---
---

**Write down the name of one person that U trust enough to help U
in these areas.**

---

Celebrate Your Resolve

"I have learned over the years that when one's mind is made up,
this diminishes fear; knowing what must be done does away with fear."

~Rosa Parks~

# CELEBRATE YOUR RESOLVE

You've made up your mind.

You've reached your decision.

It took a lot of time, overtime and prayer, but you're done with giving
more body-drained-of-energy-space to what has occupied your mind
long enough.

You've talked with enough people, sought and received more advice
than necessary and the ball has been placed in your court,
and you're ready.

You're resolved.

No longer will U be haunted or give thoughts to second guessing
what is best for U.

Today U arise with a resolve that cannot be
and will not be compromised.

Now it's time to move forward without regret.

**Assignment:**

**There's something that you've been putting off.**

**For whatever reason, over and over again,
U can't seem to find resolution.**

**It could be that U are looking for more clues or signs of something that
will change your mind,
but U must stop over-thinking your decision.**

**Once you've made your mind up, trust your judgment, make your move
and move on.**

**What one thing continues to remain in your face,
taking up unnecessary space, when you've already made up your mind.**

_______________________________________________

_______________________________________________

_______________________________________________

_______________________________________________

_______________________________________________

_______________________________________________

_______________________________________________

_______________________________________________

_______________________________________________

_______________________________________________

**Congratulations, U just took the first step!!!**

3 John 1:2
King James Version (KJV)

"Beloved, I wish above all things that thou mayest prosper
and be in health,
even as thy soul prospereth."


Celebrate Your Health


"Women in particular need to keep an eye on their physical and mental
health, because if we're scurrying to and from appointments and errands,
we don't have a lot of time to take care of ourselves.
We need to do a better job of putting ourselves higher on our own 'to do' list."

~Michelle Obama~

# CELEBRATE YOUR HEALTH


If U participate in a physical activity
like a brisk walk, a jog, sprint, lifting weights, climbing steps, aerobics,
line-dancing, rollin' on a bike, kickboxing, boot camp...

If U change your eating habits,
cutting out the bad carbs, limiting the sugar intake,
steering away from those late night snacks,
increasing the veggies, fruit and water...

Should U make an effort to get more rest
and adopt the philosophy of 'early to bed — early to rise', reduce the
amount of stress, erase the negativity and increase the positivity...

U will realize that no one,
absolutely no one,
can take care of U,
better than U.

Be a health advocate of U ~ for U.

After all,
there's only going to be one of U.

**Assignment:**

**Make a point to participate in a physical activity that gets your heart rate going and those sweat glands working.**

**(And yes, sex does count – but how about trying something that doesn't necessarily require it.)**

**Set goals for yourself.**

**Today, walk for five minutes  -  tomorrow walk for ten minutes.**

**Girl, before U know it, you'll be up to thirty minutes.**

**U know what foods U need to stay away from and those in which U should indulge more.**

**Simply do it!**

**Drink that water, cut that fat, shake less salt.**

**U can do it!**

**And at the end of your day,
allow your mind, body and soul to rest.**

**U deserve it,
after all tomorrow's coming
and U want to be around to enjoy it.**

Celebrate Your Compassion

"When we're looking for compassion,

we need someone who is deeply rooted, is able to bend and,

most of all, embraces us for our strengths and struggles."

~Brene Brown~

# CELEBRATE YOUR COMPASSION

Inside the heart of every woman there resides a nurturer.

When U witness the wrong doing of another,
hear of the difficulties of others
and even hear the cries of a nearby child,
your heart longs to help, aid and comfort.

U have the ability of coming as close to feeling what another may feel
as possible.

U long to bring back normalcy and sometimes
U find it hard to rest until all of your efforts have been exhausted.

Your heart strings are urging U to do your part to make the life of
another better and easier.

Don't try to stifle the strumming melody of your compassion.

Rather, allow it to course throughout every fiber of your being for, in
doing so, U spring into action to serve, heal and provide for another.

**Assignment:**

**Who needs your help?**

_______________________________________________

**How can U help?**

_______________________________________________

_______________________________________________

_______________________________________________

**When will U help?**

_______________________________________________

**Don't put off until tomorrow what U can do to help another today.**

Proverbs 16:31
King James Version (KJV)

"The hoary (gray) head is a crown of glory,
if it be found in the way of righteousness."


Celebrate Your Shades of Gray


"Gray hair is God's graffiti"

~Comedian Bill Cosby~

# CELEBRATE YOUR SHADES OF GRAY

The natural color and shade of your hair is either going to give way, is
giving way, or has already surrendered to your shades of gray.

U can cover them, dye them or try to hide them,
but they are there  -  your shades of gray.

They belong to U, whether U want to own them or not.

They have a mind of their own and won't be easily tamed.
Perhaps because it took them so long to arrive, therefore, they want to
run free and wild.

Don't be ashamed of them, cover them if U must,
but take ownership of them, for they are a part of U
and they have a message...

They speak of your moments spent and shared on this side of eternity
and possess wisdom that can only come with time.

**Assignment:**

**The next time that U see a gray hair,
don't be so quick to snatch it from its' roots.**

**I've heard it said that when one gray haired is snatched, two will take
its' place – so let it be.  Don't fight it  ~  welcome it!**

**Does the gray hair take away from U being U?**

**Take the time to write a prayer of thanks for that gray hair before U let
it lay or cover it up, for its' existence is a testimony
of your still being here.**

___________________________________________________

___________________________________________________

___________________________________________________

___________________________________________________

___________________________________________________

___________________________________________________

___________________________________________________

___________________________________________________

___________________________________________________

___________________________________________________

___________________________________________________

___________________________________________________

___________________________________________________

___________________________________________________

___________________________________________________

___________________________________________________

Isaiah 35:6
King James Version (KJV)

"Then shall the lame man leap…"


Celebrate Your Potholes & Hurdles

Your Jump-to-it-tiveness


"I think everybody has tragedy in their life
Everybody has hurdles in their life.
Everybody has tough things to overcome.
My kids say to me, 'This isn't fair.' I said, 'Life isn't fair.'
Everybody has their issues.
It's how you handle your issues that distinguishes you."

~Maria Shriver~

# CELEBRATE YOUR POTHOLES & HURDLES ~ YOUR JUMP-TO-IT-TIVENESS

During your journey,
the road on which you're traveling won't always be smooth.

There will be curves, hills, valleys, mountains, potholes
and even hurdles, all of which require that U possess the ability to
jump over and jump high.

The potholes in your life represent the holes that, if ignored, will cause
U to fall in, deep and hard.  They are craters of despair with the
intention of slowing your roll and even keeping U stranded
until help comes along.

The hurdles are those barriers that were put in place to keep U from
reaching your destiny.  They are of various heights and require that you
be able to jump over them and to do so takes practice.  For just as U
master the ability to conquer one hurdle, a higher one awaits.

Both of these, the pothole and the hurdle, serve different purposes.

The pothole can hold the power to destroy for if U are overcome by its
depth, U may become overwhelmed.

The hurdle can harness the power to progress,
for by overcoming, U are moving forward.

Yet, they both require that U Jump.

Do not jump into it.
Jump over it.
Jump beyond it.

Now, U can sing and teach another how to make it over.

**Assignment:**

**None of us are immune to getting caught up at one time or another.**

**Oftentimes, the frequency of the potholes and/or hurdles will be dependent upon the power that awaits U upon your arrival to your destination.**

**So, ask yourself, where are U going?**

_______________________________________________
_______________________________________________
_______________________________________________
_______________________________________________
_______________________________________________

**What do U hope to accomplish once U get there?**

_______________________________________________
_______________________________________________
_______________________________________________
_______________________________________________
_______________________________________________

**What potholes and/or hurdles have U experienced on your journey to unleash the power of U?**

_______________________________________________
_______________________________________________
_______________________________________________
_______________________________________________
_______________________________________________

*Mark 4:39*
*King James Version (KJV)*

*"And He arose, and rebuked the wind, and said unto the sea, 'Peace, be still.'*
*And the wind ceased, and there was a great calm."*

**Celebrate Your Storms**

*"Storms make trees take deeper roots."*

*~Dolly Parton~*

# CELEBRATE YOUR STORMS

There U are.

Standing.

And as U look above, U can see the storm clouds that have gathered.
The thunder roars, the lightning flashes, the wind blows and the first
raindrop splashes against your skin,
followed by a succession of raindrops that turn into a torrential storm.

Sometimes life comes along unexpectedly and during your journey,
even though U heard and listened to the weather forecast and believed
that your days ahead would yield a cloudless sky, out of no where,
U find yourself confronted with a situation, an encounter or an
experience that challenges your ability to withstand
and even continue to make progress.

This moment during your journey must be identified for what it is ~
a storm.

A storm does what storms do.
They come through, run their course and then...they depart.

Knowing this, the question is not what U are going to do <u>about</u> your
storm, but what are U going to do <u>while in the midst</u> of this storm.

Don't claim the storm as yours, as if it belongs to U for keeps,
for in claiming this storm, U are tying yourself to it.

Change your perception of the storm for it was sent to develop U,
not to destroy U.

Therefore, claim your lesson of survival and claim your victory  ~
before the storm even passes on to another, for in doing so, U are
informing this storm and all others to come that U will not be defined
nor defeated by its' existence.

Yet, while in the midst, don't fool yourself into thinking that it will be
easy, for the storms personality could be one of a destructive nature.
However, the phenomenality of who U are, can stand and will stand for
U are powerful beyond measure.

As a child, I recall riding home in a car one night with my mother and
brother,  after leaving from a visit with my grandmother.

When we left my grandmother's home, though it was dark, the stars
were twinkling in the dark blue velvet sky.

We had not been driving for more than ten minutes, when suddenly,
the stars and the glow of the moon were overcome by the black clouds.

The rain began to pellet the car, the thunder roared and the lightning
zigzagged across the sky.

The windshield wipers were working overtime in order to give my
mother a clear view of the road upon which we traveled,
as she slowly crawled through the city.

I began to think about how if we were still at my grandmother's home,
she would have us huddled in her living room, lights turned off and
voices hushed, as she reminded us to be still and quiet,
for God was at work.

Yet, here we were, trying our best to make it home.
It was if we were the only ones out and about.
It was as if everyone had received the memo of the storm,
except for us, for the streets were bare.

I was afraid.

When the thunder roared, I jumped.

When the lightning scrawled its strange language across the sky, I slid
from my seat into the floorboards of the car, perhaps thinking that the
lower I went, the safer I would be.

As the rain continued to fall, I looked over at my brother.

Instead of fear or dread, his face held a look of fascination.

Every time the lightning flashed, his smile became brighter and
brighter and his eyes twinkled with glee.

I didn't understand it.

It didn't make sense.

How could this little boy be at ease?
Of course, I too was little, but his being younger than I accounted for
something in my world.

Was he immune to what was going on around us,
I asked myself.

Suddenly, while the thunder continued to roar, my little brothers'
words filled the car, informing us of the reason for his excitement, glee
and perception of the storm as he said, "Mommy, make sure U smile
because God's taking our picture."

**Assignment:**

Storms come and storms go.
I've heard it said that U are either headed for a storm,
U are either in a storm or U are just leaving a storm.

**Where are U today?**

_______________________________________________


**Are U focusing on the storm or are U trying to salvage the lesson?**

_______________________________________________
_______________________________________________
_______________________________________________
_______________________________________________


Though this storm was necessary for your growth,
the storm does not belong to U ~ the lesson does.

**What are U learning from this storm?**

_______________________________________________
_______________________________________________
_______________________________________________
_______________________________________________
_______________________________________________
_______________________________________________

Whatever you've learned, hold it within your heart,
U just may need it for the next storm and believe me,
it's on the way.

So, enjoy the sunshine, relish the warmth of its' rays
and carry it with U in the reserve of your soul for the days to come.

*Nehemiah 8:10*

*King James Version (KJV)*

*"…the joy of the LORD is your strength."*

*Celebrate Your Joy*

*"For happiness one needs security,*
*but joy can spring like a flower even from the cliffs of despair."*

*~Anne Morrow Lindbergh~*

# CELEBRATE YOUR JOY

U are beyond happy.

U are beyond content.

U are beyond satisfied.

U have joy.

Unspeakable joy.

This joy was not given to U by anyone in this world.

Therefore, no one in the world will ever be able to take your joy away
from U.

It's a joy that was placed within the reservoirs of your soul where it
can be protected for safe keeping in those moments when U need it.

Your joy is not based on the happenings of life nor the possession of
materialistic goods, it is the wellness of your being, the fullness of your
person and the delight in knowing that U are phenomenal,
U are amazing
and that U are worth having and preserving the joy
that U possess.

U are joy personified.

**Assignment:**

**There's a popular song that says,**

**"I still have joy, I still have joy,
after all of the things I've been through I still have joy."**

**Do U still have joy?**

**If not, what have U allowed to replace your joy?**

**Grief, sorrow, pain, past mistakes, unforgiveness, resentment, bitterness?**

**Whatever it is, write it down so that U can be done with it and regain the joy that U deserve.**

____________________________________________________________

____________________________________________________________

____________________________________________________________

____________________________________________________________

____________________________________________________________

____________________________________________________________

**If your joy is intact,
there's someone who needs a shot of your joy.**

**And U know who they are.**

**Help and assist them in the rejuvenation of the joy that lies within their souls for their sake and your service.**

*1 Timothy 6:8*
*King James Version (KJV)*

*"And having food and raiment let us be therewith content."*

## Celebrate Your Palate

*"The odds of going to the store for a loaf of bread and coming out with only a loaf of bread are three billion to one."*
*~Erma Bombeck~*

# CELEBRATE YOUR PALATE

Cereal, oatmeal or grits; pancakes or waffles; bacon or sausage;
eggs that are scrambled, sunny-side up, folded as an omelet,
with cheese or without; hash browns or home-fried potatoes...

Pizza with extra cheese, or pepperoni, sausage, veggies, anchovies,
grilled chicken or the works...

Loaded baked potatoes; French fries dipped in ketchup, ranch salad
dressing or covered with cheese sauce and chili...

Cheesesteaks, hoagies, subs or wraps...

Soup or salad; sandwiches ~ half or whole...

Fried chicken, baked chicken, smothered chicken...

Ice cream with fudge, caramel  or without, or simply
a scoop by itself...

Beef or pork...Duck or pate'...Chitterlings or turkey...

Salt, pepper, ketchup, mustard, hot sauce or tabasco...

Pound cake, donuts, pies, lemon tarts, apple pie, blueberry,
cherry or peach...

It's up to U!!!

Sometimes the nose is assaulted by the aroma of food before the eyes
can see it, your clean hands touch it or your tongue gets to taste it, but
when it does...your palate is overcome with the delectable,
scrumptious delight of glorious food.

**U have an acquired taste that could never be duplicated
in thought or deed.**

**Whatever U choose to enjoy as a delectable treat,
whether it was suggested by another or an original recipe,
it's your taste.**

**Savor every bite  ~  BON APPETIT!!!**

**Assignment:**

**Today, indulge!**

**What are your favorite foods, snacks, or munchies?**

___________________________________________

___________________________________________

___________________________________________

___________________________________________

___________________________________________

___________________________________________

___________________________________________

___________________________________________

___________________________________________

**If you're on a diet,**
**take this moment to splurge on that favorite craving,**
**or that one-of-a-kind combination of flavors that when brought**
**together by U make your tongue tingle and your taste buds**
**shout for joy!!!**

**Indulge and enjoy!!!**

**U only live once!!!**

*Psalm 128:6*
*King James Version (KJV)*

*"Yea, thou shalt see thy children's children,"*

## Celebrate Your Grands

*"If I had known grandchildren were this much fun,*
*I would have had them first."*

*~Unknown~*

# CELEBRATE YOUR GRANDS

If you've been blessed with children,
they are an extension of U.

Their children are a greater extension of U,
for they reach further into time.

They are your gift for having been here and leaving the best part
of who U are.

They are your contribution to the world.

Whether they are your biological seed or not,
U are the example for them to follow.

U serve as the mother and/or grandmother that they may never have.

And guess what?
They're watching U.
They're learning from U.
So, walk with determination and purpose as a light on the journey.
Speak with wisdom and nurture with love.
Bless them with your honesty and guidance.
Pray earnestly for their care.

**Assignment:**

**Write down the names of your grands.**
**Write down their special qualities.**
**How can U continue to help them to be the best that they can be?**

**Name:**_______________________________________________________
**Qualities:**____________________________________________________
_______________________________________________________________
_______________________________________________________________

**How can U help this grandchild?**
_______________________________________________________________
_______________________________________________________________
_______________________________________________________________

**Name:**_______________________________________________________
**Qualities:**____________________________________________________
_______________________________________________________________
_______________________________________________________________

**How can U help this grandchild?**
_______________________________________________________________
_______________________________________________________________
_______________________________________________________________

**Name:**_______________________________________________________
**Qualities:**____________________________________________________
_______________________________________________________________
_______________________________________________________________

**How can U help this grandchild?**
_______________________________________________________________
_______________________________________________________________
_______________________________________________________________

**Feel free to use as much space as U need for your grands.**

*Philippians 4:7*
*King James Version (KJV)*

*"And the peace of God,*
*which passeth all understanding,*
*shall keep your hearts and minds through Christ Jesus."*

Celebrate Your Peace

*"Dear God,*
*Please send to me the spirit of Your peace.*
*Then send, dear Lord,*
*the spirit of peace from me to all the world.  Amen."*

*~Marianne Williamson~*

**CELEBRATE YOUR PEACE**


Given all that you've been through,
given all that you've experienced
and all of the things that are going on in your life right now,
one could say that U should be stressed to the max.

While others are frazzled, anxious and unsettled,
U are at ease.

When those around U holler, scream and shout with drama-filled
moments of nervousness or fear,
U are at ease.

It's not as though U are looking through rose-colored glasses or even
being unrealistic about life, but your spirit is free from any
disturbances that could wreak havoc on your soul

U are at peace.

U are at peace with who U are.
U are at peace with your purpose.
U are at peace with where U are.
U are at peace with U.

U have peace that flows like a river...
it is truly well with your soul.

**Assignment:**

**Are U at peace with U?**

**If not, why not?**

**What do U have to prove to anyone, other than yourself?**

**What will it take for U to find peace?**

_________________________________________________
_________________________________________________
_________________________________________________
_________________________________________________
_________________________________________________
_________________________________________________
_________________________________________________
_________________________________________________
_________________________________________________
_________________________________________________
_________________________________________________
_________________________________________________
_________________________________________________
_________________________________________________
_________________________________________________
_________________________________________________
_________________________________________________
_________________________________________________
_________________________________________________
_________________________________________________

**Other than your Creator, the only approval worth seeking is that of your own.**
**Let your peace flow throughout every fiber of your being, like a river.**

Job 11:17

King James Version (KJV)

"And thine age shall be clearer than the noonday:
thou shalt shine forth, thou shalt be as the morning."

Celebrate Your Age

"Don't get all weird about getting older!
Our age is merely the number of years the world has been enjoying us."

~Maxine~

# CELEBRATE YOUR AGE

When U were younger, U wanted to be older.
Now that U are older, sometimes U want to be younger.

It's time to find joy in the age in which U find yourself.

For 365 days U are blessed to be one age.

Find the blessing in each day that you receive during that one year
and make it count.

Each day will give way to a lesson.

Each week will give way to an accomplishment.

Each month will equal a triumph.

Every year will catapult U to a higher level of U.

Relish your days, weeks, months, and the year of this age.

For U shall not pass this way again.

**There's no sense in going back in age, looking for a take-back or a do-over ~ what's done is done.**

**Today, look forward to how U can find joy, peace and live each age to the fullest of your phenomenal self.**

**Write down the things that U are going to accomplish during this age ~ start with this day, follow-up with each week, move on to your monthly goals and on to this year and tackle life with fervor and an unstoppable force, after all U only have 365 days to get it done and the seconds aren't waiting for U.**

*Isaiah 58:11*
*King James Version (KJV)*

*"And the LORD shall guide thee continually,*
*and satisfy thy soul in drought, and make fat thy bones:*
*and thou shalt be like a watered garden,*
*and like a spring of water, whose waters fail not."*

## Celebrate Your Garden

*"In search of my mother's garden, I found my own."*

*~Alice Walker~*

## CELEBRATE YOUR GARDEN


At first U were simply a seed.

U had been planted deep within the earth's soil.

U received the proper nourishment in order to grow.

U burst through the soil to make your appearance and
U announced to the world that U ARE HERE!!!

U are here to continue to grow.

The growth in your life comes from every season.

Despite the harsh winter winds, U found that the flames of your desire
kept U warm.

Your winter was necessary to kill off those things that were of no
benefit to your life.

As U welcome the freshness of spring U are willing to begin anew, to
grow anew and to blossom anew.

It is during the summer months that U are in full bloom and others see
your beauty and feed from the garden of U.

The fall reminds U of the preparation to purge, once again.
To pull up the weeds that have attached themselves to U, and if given
the chance to grow, will choke the life from U.

U know that the frigid winds are sure to return, but U have no fear,
for the fire~ your fire, will forever burn inside of U until U are able to
come forth, yet again, as a phenomenal force
to be reckoned with.

**Assignment:**

**It's time to purge your life.**

**What or who needs to be purged from U?**

**Who has attached themselves to U, not to receive strength, nor to assist in your growth, but to wrap itself or themselves around the root of who U are in order to stifle and choke the very life of U?**

**Write down these things or those persons and why, not because U are tossing them from your life, but to be forever aware of them, in hopes that they will come to know their phenomenal selves.**

______________________________________________

______________________________________________

______________________________________________

______________________________________________

______________________________________________

______________________________________________

______________________________________________

______________________________________________

______________________________________________

______________________________________________

______________________________________________

**Part II:**

**What or who is helpful and needed to assist in your growth? This thing or person is not afraid of your growth but they are able to celebrate U in knowing that as U grow, they will grow, as well.**

_______________________________________________

_______________________________________________

_______________________________________________

_______________________________________________

_______________________________________________

_______________________________________________

_______________________________________________

_______________________________________________

**Part III**

**What are U willing to do in order to make your growth as consistent as possible and how can U help another to grow?**

_______________________________________________

_______________________________________________

_______________________________________________

_______________________________________________

_______________________________________________

_______________________________________________

_______________________________________________

_______________________________________________

# Celebrate Your Finish

"Getting organized in the normal routines of life and finishing little projects
you've started is an important first step toward realizing larger goals.
If you can't get a handle on the small things, how will you ever get it together
to focus on the big things?"

~Joyce Meyer~

2 Timothy 4:7
King James Version (KJV)

"I have fought a good fight,
I have finished my course,
I have kept the faith:"

"It's not who you are that holds you back,
it's who you think you're not."

~Unknown~

## CELEBRATE YOUR FINISH

It took U a while, but it's done.

U may have experienced some bumps in the road,
but U completed the task.

Some said that U would never finish.

Others doubted that U even wanted to finish.

U did it!!!

Instead of falling prey to their doubts and denials of your ability,
U finished what U started.

U can cross this item off of your to-do list for U have met your goal and
U have crossed the finish line.
And U do so with arms extended towards heaven in glorious splendor,
yet, ready yourself knowing that there is more to be done,
for your race continues.

And so, today,
U will celebrate the completion of this project
with a fierce determination as U continue to reach the conclusion of U.

**Assignment:**

**Take a good look at your to-do list...**

**What have U been putting off for completion?**

**What has been on your to-do list forever,
waiting to be scratched off of your list?**

_________________________________________________

_________________________________________________

_________________________________________________

_________________________________________________

_________________________________________________

**Today, set a time line of goals to complete what you've started.**

**Don't allow anyone or anything keep U from reaching your goal.**

**Now, those things on your to-do list that U know you're not going to tackle, maybe it sounded like a good idea at the time but now U realize that it requires more energy than it's worth ~ erase them and cross them off.**

Psalm 23:4
King James Version (KJV)

"Yea, though I walk through the valley of the shadow of death,
I will fear no evil:  for Thou art with me;
Thy rod and Thy staff they comfort me."


# Celebrate Your Valleys


"Life has all sorts of hills and valleys,
and sometimes you don't end up doing what you had your heart set on,
but sometimes that's even better"

~Comedian Ruth Buzzi~

# CELEBRATE YOUR VALLEYS

It's not easy to be in the valley.

It's not easy to find yourself in the valley.

The valley has always been portrayed as a place of darkness
and of being alone.

And here U are.

First, know that U are not alone.

Second, remember that there's a light that shines within U that adds
brightness to the darkest of situations.

Sure, we all get a bit down, depressed, in the dumps and just plain ol'
sad, and when life piles on top of U, it's easy to allow it to take U down
into the spiral of the valley.

U have one of two choices…

U can walk in fear while in this valley,
or U can make the most of your time spent while here.

Whatever U decide,
U must not stay here for many have found themselves in this place and
have lingered longer than needed.

U are in the valley to learn more about U.

U must celebrate while in the valley, dance in the darkness, pick up the
pace and make progress.

U are in the valley to become a better U.

**And once U depart,
though U will venture into another valley along your journey,
U will know how to handle it and rather than focus on the darkness,
U will know that this moment will not last forever.**

**Assignment:**

**Ok, U are here, in the valley,
and U must ask yourself some questions…**

**How did U get here?**

**U weren't born here and U are not destined to remain,
so how did U end up here?
Did someone hurt your feelings?  Were U betrayed or did U all of a
sudden decide to clothe yourself in the funk of the valley,
rather than continue to make your way through?**

———————————————————————————————

———————————————————————————————

**How long have U been here?**

**Every valley has an entrance  ~   when did U become a resident?**

———————————————————————————————

———————————————————————————————

**How long do U intend to stay?**

**Every valley has an exit ~  can U find it?**

———————————————————————————————

———————————————————————————————

**Read every answer so that U will able to better handle
the next valley excursion.**

*Psalm 144:1*
*King James Version (KJV)*

*"Blessed be the LORD my strength which teacheth my hands to war,*
*and my fingers to fight:"*


**Celebrate Your Fight**


*"I know things that are broken can be fixed. Take the punch if you have to,*
*hit the canvas and then get up again.*
*Life is worth it."*

*~Queen Latifah~*

# CELEBRATE YOUR FIGHT

There's a determination inside of U that no one can harness.

U were not meant to be harnessed, anyway,
for U are not a wild animal.

U are a phenomenal woman!!!

It's your determination that fuels U to fight when others would quit.

As U stand in the boxing ring,
looking at what stands before U,
be it another human or an undeserved fear that has crept its' way into
your space, U dare them or it to make the first move.

No one, no thing will be able to extinguish the fire of your fight.

U are willing to give and take every punch, each uppercut, the jabs,
kicks, and scratches for who U are and what U believe.

U have followed your heart and realize that this fight, unlike others,
is one worth fighting

This is your fight, this is your battle.

U chose to fight this knowing that whether battered, bruised or bloody,
it was worth it, for U are, already, the victor.

**Assignment:**

**What moral conviction or what cause do U believe
is worth fighting for?**

______________________________________________

______________________________________________

______________________________________________

______________________________________________

______________________________________________

______________________________________________

______________________________________________

______________________________________________

______________________________________________

**Have U wasted any of your precious time,
fighting a battle that was not yours to fight?**

______________________________________________

**If so, reevaluate your stance and retreat, not as a result of fear of the
fight, but in order to rededicate energy and time
to the rediscovery of U!**

*Hebrews 11:1*
*King James Version (KJV)*

*"Now faith is the substance of things hoped for,*
*the evidence of things not seen."*


*Celebrate Your Faith*


*"Without faith, nothing is possible.  With faith, nothing is impossible."*

*~Mary McCloud Bethune~*

# CELEBRATE YOUR FAITH

Sometimes your faith is the only thing upon which U can stand.

It is your deep rooted belief in the unseen and the confidence
in the unknown.

It is the unfailing affirmation that no matter what happens, no matter
what transpires, and regardless of where U are,
that all is well.

Your faith conquers your fears, for the two can never co-exist.
Therefore, U must feed your faith and starve your fears.

Your faith is to trust in your Almighty God which fuels the amount of
faith that U have in yourself in order to accomplish, to do and to be
more than what U have become, to be more than what others may
perceive and to transcend the possibilities of your own imagination.

It is your faith that inspires U to walk in your greatness and demands
your complete trust to step without knowing where the path will lead,
to reach out and grab what U are unable to see and to embrace the
assured promise of your tomorrow before it arrives.

It is your everlasting hope that churns within your spirit.

It is the evidence of what U cannot see, yet U know that it is there,
pushing U, encouraging U, comforting U while it affirms and authorizes
that your hope is not in vain.

Your faith doesn't second guess, question or even ask why, it simply
knows that what is done is for the betterment of U and that in all
things, U will be sustained.

**Assignment:**

**What is your definition of faith?**

_______________________________________________

_______________________________________________

_______________________________________________

_______________________________________________

**What fears have hindered U from stepping out on faith?**

_______________________________________________

_______________________________________________

_______________________________________________

_______________________________________________

_______________________________________________

_______________________________________________

**Today, how will U feed your faith, therefore starving your fears?**

_______________________________________________

_______________________________________________

_______________________________________________

_______________________________________________

**Each day U will encounter experiences where your faith will be tested and challenged.  Today, allow your faith to grow and to soar to the hilltops of glory.**

**Live by faith…anything else would be uncivilized.**

# Celebrate Your Love

"I have decided to stick with love.
Hate is too great a burden to bear."

~Martin Luther King, Jr.~


1 Corinthians 13:13
King James Version (KJV)

"And now abideth faith, hope, charity, these three;
but the greatest of these is charity."


"Love is the greatest gift that God has given us. It's free."

~Taraji P. Henson~

## CELEBRATE YOUR LOVE

Love starts with U.
The ability to love another will coincide with the depth of love that U
have for yourself.
When U learn to genuinely love U, then U will be able to breach the
boundaries of genuinely loving another.

Love is given and received.
When U give of your love, it is deep and strong.
When U receive love, it becomes a part of U.

It is for this reason that U have learned to never use this word lightly.
After all, love is not to be tossed around with the slightest of breezes
or the shifting of temperatures.

It is a living, breathing and active phenomenon.

For to do so,
to love, unconditionally, goes against the natural human response.
It's a higher form of love because it is given freely, without hidden
agendas or manipulation.
It is powerful because it accepts one for who they are, encourages the
power of possibility and embraces the finality.

And with every day that U are given,
U are moving closer and closer to the perfection of love as U allow it
infiltrate your mind, body and soul.

U deserve the best of love,
the promise for love,
the desire to love and
U possess the power to love.

**For U know that when all else fails, when others may even come,
go or remain, it is your love
first for your God,
second for yourself,
and then passed on to others that will stand.**

**Assignment:**

**The depth of your love and your ability to love is dependent upon how U were loved and how U received it.**

**Today, remember that someone loved U first, in the creation of U ~ blessing U with the opportunity and the authority to love yourself and others.**

**Today, simply love.**

**Don't question it,
don't think too hard
or even try to figure it out,
just love.**

**Let those who are dear to U know that U love them.**

**Tell them today, not tomorrow.**

# Celebrate Your Todays

"…we've got to seize this moment, and we have to seize it soon."

~President Barack Obama~


Psalm 118:24
King James Version (KJV)

" This is the day which the LORD hath made;
we will rejoice and be glad in it."


"Sooner or later, I hate to break it to you, you're gonna die,
so how do you fill in the space between here and there?
It's yours. Seize your space."

~Margaret Atwood~

# CELEBRATE YOUR TODAYS

From this day forward,

U will celebrate every day.

For every day is a gift.

And as the day passes, it's a gift that shall never be received again.

Knowing this, celebrate every today.

Not yesterday, for it's already gone.

Not tomorrow, for it has yet to arrive.

Celebrate today.

Relish in the existence of your today.

Embrace the moments of your today.

Be thankful for your involvement in today.

It belongs to U.

It was given to U.

It was made for U.

From this day forward,

Celebrate every today.

**Assignment:**


**Live for today!!!**

**Promise yourself that from this day forward, U will live each day as if it were your last.**

**It was designed with U in mind!!!**

**May your todays, tomorrows and every moment in between be filled
with enough love to last a lifetime,
joy that cannot be measured or contained,
the empowerment to make a positive change,
and the celebration of the Father's most remarkable creation  ~  U!**


**~Debb Houston~**

**Deborah R. Houston wants to hear from you!!!**

**Choose a celebration moment in your devotional workbook and share with her and others how you took the time to Celebrate U!**
**Your Celebrate U! moment could be placed on her web site:**

**www.deborahrhouston.com**

**Deborah R. Houston provides resources for women in order to assist them in the rediscovery of their greatness and empower them to walk in their purpose.**

**She believes in nurturing the inner woman, therefore, making an impact outwardly.**

**Deborah R. Houston believes that as we embrace the gift of life and grow with each experience that we encounter, it is our responsibility to leave a positive impression on the lives of everyone, while grasping the hand of another during our journey on the path of greatness.**

**Deborah R. Houston is available for workshops, classes, training, seminars and lectures that deal with the empowerment of women of all ages.**

**Some of her areas of expertise include:**
**Celebrate U ! ~ The Phenomenality of U!**

**STYLE On The Inside**

**The Empowerment**

**Abandonment & Abuse**

**Just to name a few.**

**In order to book her services today, visit her web site.**

20349773R10127

Made in the USA
San Bernardino, CA
07 April 2015